CW00855015

D-Day: 58
Facts For Kids

David Railton

This book is just one of a series of "Fascinating Facts For Kids" books. For more fascinating facts about people, history, animals and much more please visit:

www.fascinatingfactsforkids.com

Contents

The Road to War

1.   When World War One ended in 1918 with the defeat of Germany, the country lay in ruins. The victorious nations - Britain, the United States, and France - punished Germany by taking land, imposing a huge fine, and forbidding the rebuilding of the German Army and Navy.

2.   The war had left millions of Germans with no job or money, and now they were angry at the punishment imposed on their country. But a former soldier called Adolf Hitler offered them a solution to their problems.

Adolf Hitler

3. Adolf Hitler was the leader of a political party called the National Socialists, or "Nazis," and he promised to make Germany great again if the people voted for him.

4. Hitler came to power in 1933 and set about rebuilding the Army to go to war again. He planned to build a German empire, called the "Third Reich," which he said would last for 1,000 years.

5. In 1936, Hitler's Army took control of the Rhineland, the area separating France and Germany. Two years later Austria and part of Czechoslovakia were invaded. But when Hitler invaded Poland in 1939, Britain and France declared war on Germany and World War Two began.

German occupied territories

6. Countries from all over the world would eventually become involved in World War Two. On one side were the Axis powers, led by Germany, Japan, and Italy; and on the other side were the Allies, which included Britain, France, and eventually the United States.

The United States Enters the War

7.   Britain and France were no match for Hitler's powerful Army as German soldiers stormed through Denmark, Norway, Belgium, Luxembourg, and the Netherlands. By the summer of 1940, France had been conquered and most of western Europe was under German rule. Following the fall of France, Britain stood alone against the might of the German Army.

8.   Winston Churchill, the British prime minister, tried to persuade the United States president, Franklin Roosevelt, to send American soldiers to help Britain in the fight against Hitler. Roosevelt was reluctant to send an army across the Atlantic to Europe, but he did help by providing Britain with planes, tanks, and weapons.

Winston Churchill   *Franklin Roosevelt*

9. On the other side of the world, Japan wanted to build an empire in the Pacific region, but the powerful United States Navy stood in her way, so a plan was devised to destroy the American fleet.

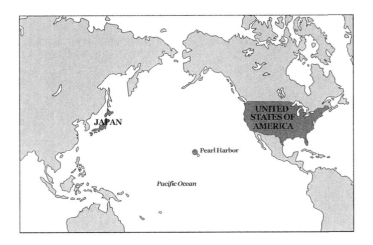

10. The headquarters of the American Navy was at Pearl Harbor, a massive naval base on one of the Hawaiian Islands in the middle of the Pacific Ocean. On the morning of December 7, 1941, the Japanese launched a surprise air attack on the American fleet, causing terrible damage and loss of life.

USS Arizona after the Japanese attack

11. The United States was outraged by the attack on Pearl Harbor, and declared war on Japan. As a fellow Axis power, Germany then declared war on the United States. This was great news for Britain, as she now had the most powerful nation on Earth fighting beside her.

12. America became a war machine, with factories churning out thousands of airplanes, warships, and weapons. Huge numbers of young men enlisted in the Army, Navy and Air Force, keen to join the fight against Hitler. In 1942, America began to send hundreds of thousands of soldiers across the Atlantic Ocean to prepare for the invasion of Nazi-controlled Europe.

The Atlantic Wall

13. It would not be easy to launch an invasion of mainland Europe from Britain. Hitler knew that the whole coastline of western Europe was vulnerable to attack, and so he had ordered the construction of a massive system of coastal defenses. It was called the "Atlantic Wall."

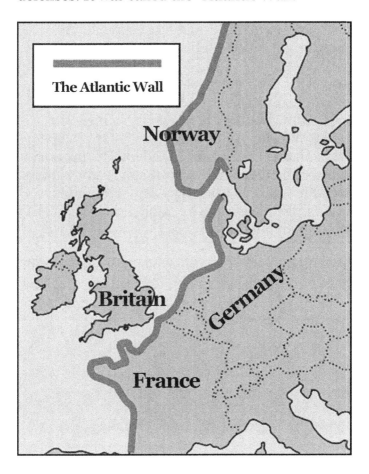

14. The building of the Atlantic Wall began in 1942, and it took two years to complete. It stretched from northern Norway all the way to the south of France - a distance of more than 2,500 miles (4,000 km).

15. The Atlantic Wall was built by hundreds of thousands of workers, many of them prisoners of war, who laid six million mines all along the coastline, each one designed to explode the moment an Allied soldier stepped on it.

16. All kinds of obstacles were placed along the coastline. Steel spikes were driven into the sand to gash the bottoms of any boats sailing over them. Wooden posts with mines on their tops were planted in the seabed to blow up any boat that came into contact with them. If any soldiers made it onto the beach they would face mile upon mile of barbed wire, more mines, and a hail of German bullets.

17. Concrete fortifications of all sizes were built behind the beaches and on top of cliffs, each one housing massive guns which pointed on to the beaches and out to sea.

Atlantic Wall fortifications

18. The Atlantic Wall was a massive project and its purpose was to stop any attempt at invasion by wiping out Allied soldiers before they could get off the beaches. Hitler believed that he had made Europe unconquerable.

Planning and Preparation

19. In May 1942, President Roosevelt and Prime Minister Churchill decided that the invasion of Europe would begin in the spring of 1944, giving them two years to plan the operation and to train and prepare their soldiers. They also had to decide which part of the European coastline the Army would go ashore at.

20. The most obvious place to start the invasion was the port of Calais, which is just over twenty miles (33 km) from the British coast. Hitler, though, would also be expecting an attack there, and the Allies needed to take the Germans by surprise.

21. The Allies chose the beaches of Normandy in northern France as the location to begin the invasion. Although it was 100 miles (160 km) across the English Channel from Britain, it had the advantage of long, flat, sandy beaches that would be perfect for landing troops from the sea.

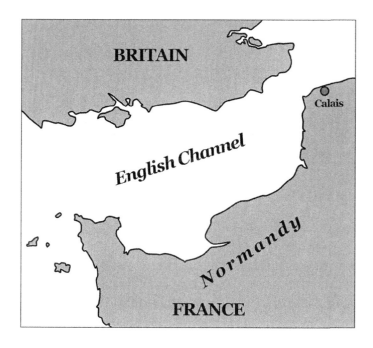

22. To get all the information they could about the landing site, the Allies sent planes to take photographs of every part of the Normandy coast, so that maps could be drawn and models made. There was even an appeal to members of the public to send in any photographs or postcards they had from visits to the area before the war!

23. An American general, Dwight Eisenhower, was chosen to be Supreme Commander of the invasion forces. He appointed a British general, Bernard Montgomery, as his second-in-command.

Eisenhower   **Montgomery**

24. Eisenhower and Montgomery devised a plan for the invasion. As it was vital to take the Germans by surprise, the first wave of soldiers would sail across the English Channel at night, under cover of darkness, to land on the beaches at dawn.

25. Hours before the landings took place, thousands of soldiers would be flown from Britain to parachute into France. Behind enemy lines, these paratroopers would try to capture roads and bridges so that the Germans could not bring in extra soldiers and weapons when the invasion started.

26. Five stretches of coastline were chosen as landing sites. Each of the beaches had a code name - *Utah*, *Omaha*, *Gold*, *Juno,* and *Sword*. The Americans would capture *Utah* and *Omaha*, the Canadians would take *Juno*, and the British targets would be *Gold* and *Sword*.

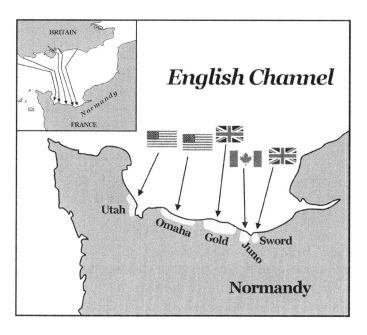

27. Eisenhower trained his men hard. They practiced crawling under barbed wire and climbing cliffs. They practiced using their weapons and equipment until they could do it in the dark, and they had to memorize maps of Normandy.

28. Soldiers from the United States and Canada were constantly arriving in Britain. Soon there were 1.7 million Americans, a million British and Canadians, and 300,000 soldiers from other countries, all training for the invasion in the countryside and on the coastline of southern England.

Operation Bodyguard

29. Eisenhower knew that if the Germans found out where and when the invasion would take place, then the element of surprise would be lost. Hitler would be able send thousands of soldiers to the landing sites to wipe out the Allies as they came ashore. A plan was made to make Hitler believe that the invasion would take place elsewhere - the plan was code-named "Operation Bodyguard."

30. In order to make Hitler think that the invasion would take place at Calais, the Allies constructed a fake army base at the port of Dover, directly across the English Channel from Calais.

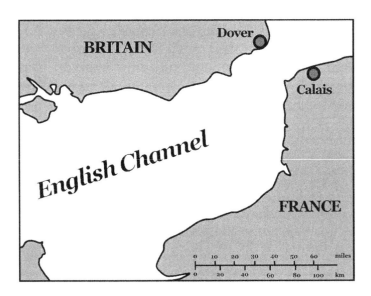

31. Hundreds of dummy tanks were made from inflatable rubber and positioned in surrounding fields and along roads. Fake trucks, jeeps, and planes filled the pretend Army base, and phoney landing craft filled the rivers and docks. Any German spy plane flying over Dover would see the "Army base," and believe that a huge invasion was about to be launched at Calais.

An inflatable dummy tank

32. The Allies also planned to make the Germans believe that a second invasion would take place in northern Europe. British radio operators in Scotland broadcast messages ordering huge numbers of skis and cold-weather equipment. When the Germans overheard the broadcasts they would assume an invasion would take place in Norway, 250 miles (400 km) across the North Sea from Britain.

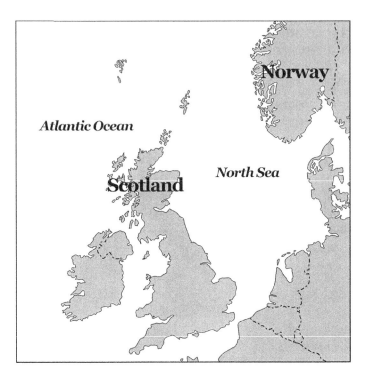

33. In order to make Operation Bodyguard even more believable, the British captured German spies stationed in England. These spies were given the choice of working for the Allies or being executed for espionage.

34. Most of the German spies chose to be double agents, working for the Allies but appearing to the Germans to be still acting for them. The spies sent messages back to Germany reporting the preparations for an attack on Calais.

35. Operation Bodyguard was a huge success. Hitler was fooled into thinking that the invasion would come at Calais and Norway. He sent extra troops to Norway, and made sure his best army was surrounding Calais, far from the beaches of Normandy.

The Invasion Begins

36. General Eisenhower wanted calm seas, a full moon, and cloudless skies for the invasion, and he asked weather experts to forecast the most suitable days in either May or June of 1944. June 5 - known as "D-Day" - was chosen, and Eisenhower ordered his ships to prepare to sail.

37. Hundreds of thousands of men had gathered across southern England, and thousands of ships were waiting to take them across the English Channel to Normandy. It would be the largest invasion by sea in history.

38. On June 3, the invasion fleet was waiting off the southern coast of England, fully loaded with men and machines waiting to go into battle. But the next morning Eisenhower was told that a huge storm was blowing in over Normandy that would last for days.

39. Eisenhower took the decision to postpone the invasion and hope for better weather. Getting his soldiers back off the ships would cause massive disruption and delays, so he ordered his men to stay on board, where they battled boredom and seasickness in the heavy seas.

40. Later that day it looked as though there could be a break in the weather on June 6. Eisenhower had a big decision to make. Delaying the invasion meant that the Germans might find out about it, whereas sailing in a storm put the success of the attack at risk. Eisenhower took a gamble and gave the command, "Okay, let's go."

Invasion by Air

41. The D-Day invasion began with an airborne attack. Hundreds of planes took off from England just after midnight on June 6, carrying a total of 20,000 paratroopers to Normandy. Their mission was to capture important roads and bridges, and disrupt German communications.

Paratroopers just before takeoff

42. When they reached Normandy ninety minutes later, the planes came under heavy fire from anti-aircraft guns on the ground. The German onslaught was so severe that it was safer to jump out of the aircraft rather than stay on board and risk being shot down.

43. Even though they were a long way from where they were supposed to land, thousands of paratroopers jumped from their planes. Many were killed by German gunfire before they reached the ground, and the men who survived landed in fields, trees, and rivers - miles from their intended targets.

44. Despite being lost in the dark and confused after their scattered landing, many paratroopers were able to meet up and organize themselves into fighting forces. They bravely fought German soldiers and were able to seize vital bridges and roads.

45. Around one in five paratroopers were killed, injured, or captured during the attack, but the bravery they showed gave the Allies their first victory of D-Day and prepared the way for the land invasion.

The Land Invasion

46. The largest invasion fleet ever seen reached a point twelve miles (19 km) from the Normandy coast in the early hours of June 6, having crossed the English Channel under cover of darkness. 155,000 soldiers were waiting to go ashore.

47. Thousands of soldiers began climbing down rope nets hanging over the sides of their ships and into small landing craft that would take them to the shore. Heavy tanks and other vehicles also made the trip ashore in specially built landing craft.

48. The trip to the shore was not pleasant. The rough seas made many men seasick, and they were soaked to the skin as six-foot waves crashed into their boats. Many tanks were lost as the heavy seas filled the landing craft with water before sinking.

49. As the boats sailed towards the Normandy coast, hundreds of Allied aircraft flew overhead to drop their bombs on German defenses. Out at sea, more than thirty battleships pounded the fortifications with shells.

A battleship pounds the shore

50. The first boats arrived at the Normandy beaches at 6.30 a.m., just after sunrise. First to land were the Americans at *Utah* and *Omaha* beaches, followed by the British at *Gold*. The Canadians then landed at *Juno* before the second British force came ashore at *Sword* at 7.30 a.m.

US soldiers approaching Omaha beach

51. At *Utah*, American soldiers waded onto shore from their landing craft and found little opposition from the Germans. By the end of the day 23,000 men and 1,700 vehicles had landed at *Utah*. They were able to advance four miles (6 km) inland, suffering around 200 casualties.

Wading ashore at Utah beach

52. *Omaha* was the most difficult beach to capture, and it saw the bloodiest battle. From the tops of 100-foot-high (30-m) cliffs, the Germans were able to gun down American troops as they waded out of the water on to the beach.

53. The men who made it ashore at *Omaha* faced barbed wire, mines, and more bullets. They had nowhere to go - the five exits from the beach were all defended by the Germans. Soon, the sand and sea were red with blood, and dead bodies were everywhere.

54. Many officers had been killed in the first hour of the battle, and the surviving soldiers were looking for leadership. Brave individual soldiers stepped forward and took control of small groups of men. Destroyers out at sea were given orders to shell the German cliff-top positions, and slowly the soldiers at *Omaha* started to take control.

55. By midday, the Americans were beginning to win the battle and by nightfall, 30,000 troops had landed at *Omaha*. More than 2,000 men had been killed or wounded, but the battle for *Omaha* beach had been won.

56. To the east of *Utah* and *Omaha* beaches, British and Canadian troops landed at *Gold*, *Juno* and *Sword*. The British suffered few casualties at *Gold*, but 1,200 Canadians were killed or injured out of the 21,400 troops who landed at *Juno*. *Sword* was captured by the British after just three hours of fighting.

British troops on Sword beach

57. At the end of the first day of the invasion, all five beaches and fifty miles (80 km) of coastline had been captured at the cost of around 9,000 Allied casualties. It had been a victory that would bring the end of World War Two closer, and was the first step in liberating tens of millions of people living under Nazi control.

58. In the days that followed D-Day, hundreds of thousands more Allied troops landed in France and began the long march towards Germany. Eleven months later Germany finally surrendered and Europe was free again.

For more fascinating facts about people,
history, animals and much more please visit:

www.fascinatingfactsforkids.com

Illustration Attributions

Title Page
US Coast Guard, photo 26-G-2517

Cover
National Archives and Records Administration
[Public domain]

Adolf Hitler
Bundesarchiv, Bild 183-S33882 / CC BY-SA 3.0
DE

Winston Churchill
British Government [Public domain]

Franklin Roosevelt
www.goodfreephotos.com

USS Arizona after the Japanese attack
Photographer: Unknown Retouched by: Mmxx
[Public domain]

Paratroopers just before take-off
Department of Defense [Public domain]

A battleship pounds the shore
Royal Navy official photographer, McNeill, M H
A (Lt)

British troops on Sword beach
Knight (Capt), No 5 Army Film & Photographic
Unit [Public domain]

Printed in Great Britain
by Amazon